GET INFORMED, STAY INFORMED

CLIMATE CHANGE

Heather C. Hudak

CRABTREE
PUBLISHING COMPANY
WWW.CRABTREEBOOKS.COM

Author: Heather C. Hudak
Series research and development: Reagan Miller
Editor-in-chief: Lionel Bender
Editor: Ellen Rodger
Proofreaders: Laura Booth, Wendy Scavuzzo
Project coordinator: Petrice Custance
Design and photo research: Ben White
Production: Kim Richardson
Print coordinator: Katherine Berti
Consultant: Emily Drew, The New York Public Library

Produced for Crabtree Publishing Company by Bender Richardson White

Photographs and reproductions:
Alamy:
Bernd Lauter: p. 29
dpa picture alliance: p. 40–41
Richard Levine p. 8–9
US Senate: p. 10–11
Getty Images
Anthony Harvey: p. 38–39
Axel Schmidt/AFP: p. 14–15
China News Service: p. 26–27 (top)
David McNew: p. 24–25
Jacques Demarthon: p. 20–21
Kevin Frayer/Stringer: p. 16–17
Magazine Mothers Milk Inc: p. 36–37
Sergey Anisimov/Anadolu Agency: p. 31
NASA: p. 1
Shutterstock: box icons, cover, heading band
Ammit Jack: p. 34
arindambanerjee: p. 30
GaudiLab: p. 10
Gorodenkoff: p. 12–13
Jacob Lund: p. 9
Jan Martin Will: p. 21
KorradolYamsatthm: p. 28–29
Krista Kennell: p. 18 (bottom)
manine99: p. 34–35
Mark Fisher: p. 6–7
Martchan: p. 18 (top)
Monkey Business Images: p. 42–43
Paul Fleet: p. 32–33
rawpixel.com: p. 22–23
Richard Whitcombe: p. 32
Rob Crandall: p. 4–5
Sk Hasan Ali: p. 18–19
Stuart Monk: p. 39
Vadim Petrakov: p. 26–27 (bottom)
Diagrams: Stefan Chabluk, using the following as sources of data: p. 7 NASA, NOAA, Hadley Center, Japanese Meteorological Agency; p. 11 Pew Research Agency; p. 12 The Climate Reality Project; p. 16 NASA; p. 18 Washington Post/Remote Sensing Systems; p. 23 Pew Research Center; p. 25 Computer Engineering Research Group, University of Toronto; p. 37, 43 Pew Research Center

Library and Archives Canada Cataloguing in Publication

Hudak, Heather C., 1975-, author
Climate change / Heather C. Hudak.

(Get informed--stay informed)
Includes bibliographical references and index.
Issued in print and electronic formats.
ISBN 978-0-7787-4959-2 (hardcover).--
ISBN 978-0-7787-4970-7 (softcover).--
ISBN 978-1-4271-2119-6 (HTML)

1. Climatic changes--Juvenile literature. 2. Climate change mitigation--Juvenile literature. I. Title.

QC903.15.H83 2018 j363.738'74 C2018-903037-2
C2018-903038-0

Library of Congress Cataloging-in-Publication Data

Names: Hudak, Heather C., 1975- author.
Title: Climate change / Heather C. Hudak.
Description: New York, New York : Crabtree Publishing, [2019] | Series: Get informed-stay informed | Includes bibliographical references and index.
Identifiers: LCCN 2018033710 (print) | LCCN 2018034466 (ebook) | ISBN 9781427121196 (Electronic) | ISBN 9780778749592 (hardcover) | ISBN 9780778749707 (pbk.)
Subjects: LCSH: Climatic changes--Juvenile literature. | Climatic changes--Effect of human beings on--Juvenile literature. | Climatic changes--Government policy--Juvenile literature. | Global warming--Juvenile literature. | Nature--Effect of human beings on--Juvenile literature.
Classification: LCC QC903.15 (ebook) | LCC QC903.15 .H83 2019 (print) | DDC 363.738/74--dc23
LC record available at https://lccn.loc.gov/2018033710

Crabtree Publishing Company
www.crabtreebooks.com 1-800-387-7650

Printed in the U.S.A./102018/CG20180810

Published in Canada
Crabtree Publishing
616 Welland Ave.
St. Catharines, ON
L2M 5V6

Published in the United States
Crabtree Publishing
PMB 59051
350 Fifth Avenue, 59th Floor
New York, NY 10118

Published in the United Kingdom
Crabtree Publishing
Maritime House
Basin Road North, Hove
BN41 1WR

Published in Australia
Crabtree Publishing
3 Charles Street
Coburg North
VIC, 3058

CONTENTS

1 GLOBAL IMPACT

From intense **droughts** to devastating hurricanes and rising sea levels, **climate** change has an impact on every corner of the globe. Climate change is the long-term shift in Earth's global climate due mainly to human activity. As Earth's climate continues to warm, people and **ecosystems** face growing risks to their health and safety. According to DARA International, a nonprofit organization that assesses the impact of humanitarian aid, more than 400,000 people die each year from hunger and disease due to climate change. No person, animal, or plant is untouched by the issue.

▼ In April 2017, tens of thousands of people seeking action against climate change took part in the People's Climate March at the Capitol Building in Washington, D.C.

"A ruined planet cannot sustain human lives in good health. A healthy planet and healthy people are two sides of the same coin."

Dr. Margaret Chan, Executive Director of the World Health Organization (WHO)

QUESTIONS TO ASK

Within this book are three types of boxes with questions to help your critical thinking about climate change. The icons will help you identify them.

THE CENTRAL ISSUES
Learning about the main points of information.

WHAT'S AT STAKE
Helping you determine how the issue will affect you.

ASK YOUR OWN QUESTIONS
Prompts to address gaps in your understanding.

EVIDENCE OF CHANGE

Climate change is always making headlines in the news and on the Internet. You have likely heard stories about how climate change affects our world. You may even have noticed some of the effects of climate change in your community. And every year or two, nations from around the world meet to exchange scientific evidence and reports of government actions related to climate change, and establish new programs to combat it.

Across the globe, there is more pollution in the air from industry, transportation, and agriculture. In some parts of the world, food crops and water supplies people and animals need to live are declining. In other places, extreme heat and stronger storms are causing death and destruction. Climate change can cause animal **migration** patterns to shift, trees to flower sooner than they should, and glaciers to melt.

UNDERSTANDING THE ISSUE

You may be wondering how climate change started and what people are doing to stop it. Perhaps you are looking for ways you can be part of the solution. To answer these questions, you need to get informed about the issue.

Learning about climate change can be a big and scary task. There is a lot of information available and it is constantly being updated, revised, and reinterpreted. It is important to become an informed citizen so you understand the facts about climate change and the impact it has on the world.

LEARNERS FOR LIFE

You may think reading news about global events is something only adults need to do. But everyone, no matter their age, has a responsibility to become informed about **current affairs** and play a part in society. At school, you learn the **fundamentals** of language, mathematics, and science. However, to truly understand the world you live in, you need to open your mind to learning outside of school, as well.

Our world is always changing. History-making events take place every day. New technologies and ways of doing things are being invented all the time. Scientists are always establishing new facts and theories. Experts, government officials, and politicians are constantly reviewing and revising their opinions and statements on issues. Lifelong learners are curious about world issues and open to seeing the world in a new way.

KEEPING CURRENT

Climate change is one of the most pressing issues our planet faces today, but there is a lot of **controversy** about this issue. For years, scientists have **debated** whether human activity is causing Earth's climate to change faster than it normally would. Today, studies show 97 percent of scientists agree that it is. However, many people still have different **perspectives** about the impact of climate change and scientists are always discovering new information.

Having incorrect or outdated information puts you at risk of making poor decisions. You may assume that what was once true remains true today. Understanding how issues shift helps you develop a balanced view of the world and lets you see how people's actions and events around the world have and impact on you.

> *"Do I believe there is something called climate change? I do. Do I think that human beings affect it? I do. How much? Not enough for me to go out and cost somebody their job."*
>
> John Kasich, governor of Ohio.

THE CENTRAL ISSUES

Why do some people believe human activity does not affect climate change? How may this affect the way they solve the problem? How does staying informed about the facts help your understanding of the issue?

▼ People line up for water at a spring in Cape Town, South Africa. A drought since 2015 has threatened to drain the city's water supply—meaning taps could some day be turned off.

▼ Global surface temperatures have risen since the 1940s, but have increased even more in the last 30 years.

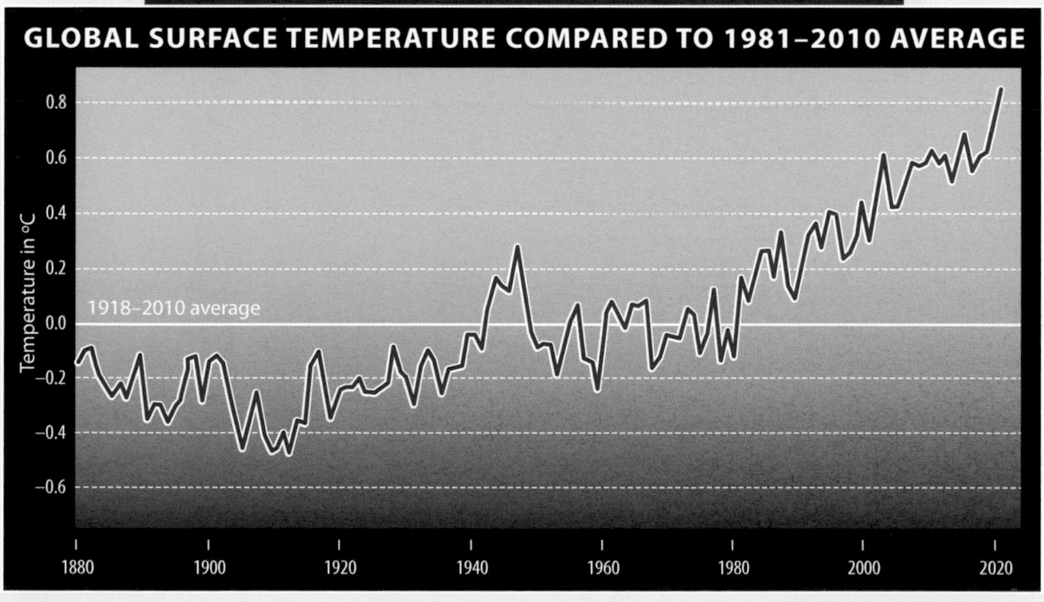

2 APPROACHING AN ISSUE

Learning about current affairs can help you gain insight into different perspectives on a subject and how to handle information. You can begin to build more informed opinions as you gain exposure to a variety of **interpretations** of events and issues. You can use what you learn to take action to improve your life and the lives of others around the world. Before you can form your own opinions and engage in conversation about a topic, you need to get informed about it.

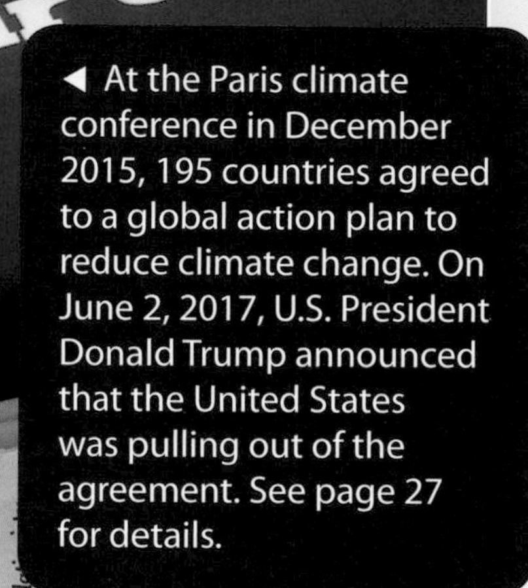

◀ At the Paris climate conference in December 2015, 195 countries agreed to a global action plan to reduce climate change. On June 2, 2017, U.S. President Donald Trump announced that the United States was pulling out of the agreement. See page 27 for details.

▼ Libraries are good places to search for background information on climate change. They often have a wide variety of source materials such as newspapers, magazines, books, almanacs, and encyclopedias.

BACKGROUND INFORMATION

It is important to learn about and develop an understanding of key background information about the topic or issue. Background information includes its history, with details of major events, their locations, dates, and the people involved. It tells you about the current status of the topic and provides **context** for its place in society. Context is the surroundings and everything that is happening alongside the topic. Background information also provides explanations of key concepts and jargon or technical words that you can use to further research the topic.

BUILDING AN UNDERSTANDING

Climate change is not a new phenomenon. French physicist Joseph Fourier first described the **greenhouse effect**—the warming effect of Earth's **atmosphere**—in 1824. Since then, countless other scientists have been researching how climate change occurs and its impact on our planet. Today, celebrities, activists, and governments are just a few of the additional key players in the ongoing discussion about climate change. Many support efforts to combat the negative impact it has on our world. Others do not believe the **hype**. Some have denied that climate change exists or is accelerated by human activities. Once you have built up your understanding of the topic, you can begin to build a vocabulary around it and start asking your own questions.

Stores of information about a topic are known as source materials. Primary source materials are firsthand accounts of events and activities based on personal experiences. They include reports written by scientists who research the effects **fossil fuels** have on the atmosphere and climate **statistics** from all over the world.

Secondary sources of information are made by **analyzing** and interpreting primary sources. A magazine article **summarizing** different scientific reports on climate change is an example of a secondary source. It may include quotes and references to the original reports.

Tertiary sources are made by compiling information from both primary and secondary sources. Encyclopedias, almanacs, and Wikipedia articles on **global warming** are tertiary sources.

WHERE TO LOOK AND LISTEN

The following are all source materials, with examples related to climate change:

- Diaries—notebooks in which people write about their personal life experiences, e.g., a farmer writing how drought affects his crops
- Photographs—e.g., newspaper images of homes destroyed by a hurricane
- Emails—messages written and delivered via a computer system, e.g., a politician's summary about the impact of global warming
- Artifacts—objects made by humans that have historical importance, e.g., primitive buildings found at Ice Age settlements
- Blogs—websites containing data about a person's **observations**, e.g., scientists' descriptions of their air-quality tests
- Podcasts—audio files downloaded to a mobile device, e.g., commentaries from a conference.

THE CENTRAL ISSUES

Primary sources are made by people who have performed research or experienced an event. Why may they be more reliable and accurate than secondary or tertiary sources? Why is it important to use all three types of sources as background information?

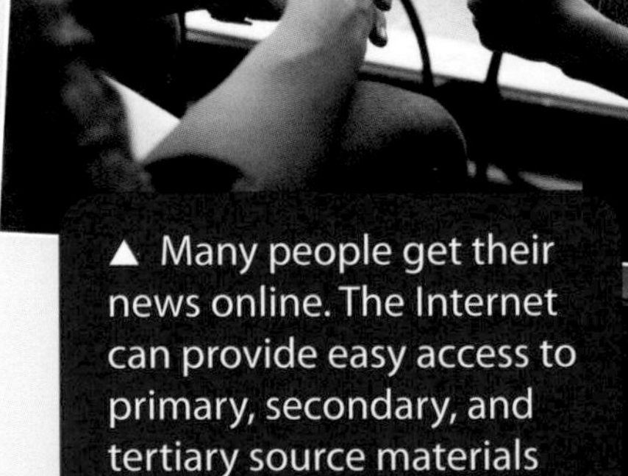

▲ Many people get their news online. The Internet can provide easy access to primary, secondary, and tertiary source materials about climate change.

WHERE AMERICAN ADULTS GET THEIR NEWS

	18–29	30–49	50–64	65+
TV	27%	45%	72%	85%
Online	50%	49%	29%	20%
Radio	14%	27%	29%	24%
Print	5%	10%	23%	48%

Age groups

Figures for each age group who often get their news from several media sources.

▼ Many people use social media platforms to share their perspectives on the world. In February 2017, U.S. Senator Bernie Sanders (seated left) and Bill Nye (right) the "Science Guy" hosted a Facebook Live session to express their views on climate change.

FACT OR FICTION?

Because "fake news" is becoming common, you must ensure your source materials are **credible**. Fake news is not based on facts but is presented as if it is. Credible sources contain facts based on historical **evidence** and scientific research. Some sources contain **myths**, misconceptions, or inaccurate details. A person may see record-breaking snowfalls and claim they are proof Earth's climate is not actually warming. However, increases in global temperatures have been recorded worldwide.

Some source materials have clear bias: They have a strong prejudice for or against something. The bias may result from personal opinion instead of facts, or because the creator wants to encourage you to buy their product. As a result, the material may not be a reliable source of information.

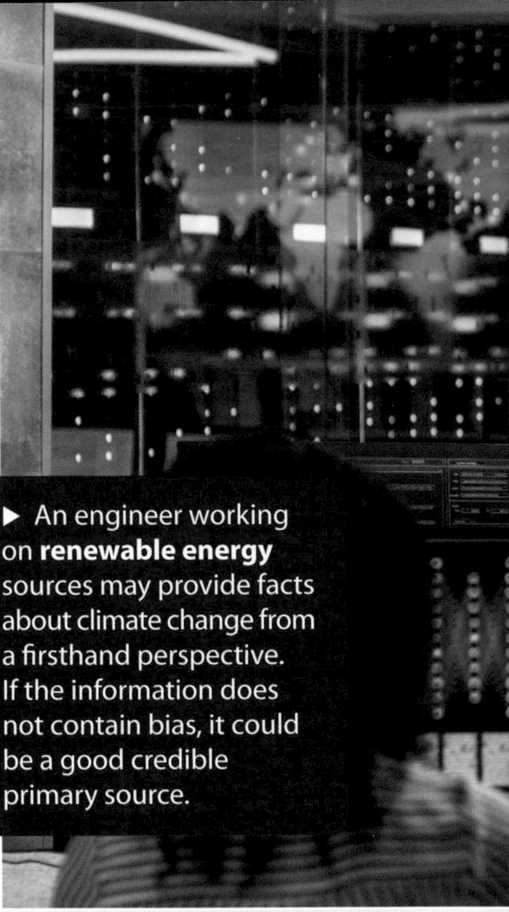

▶ An engineer working on **renewable energy** sources may provide facts about climate change from a firsthand perspective. If the information does not contain bias, it could be a good credible primary source.

Sources: www.epa.gov/ghgemissions/sources-greenhouse-gas-emissions

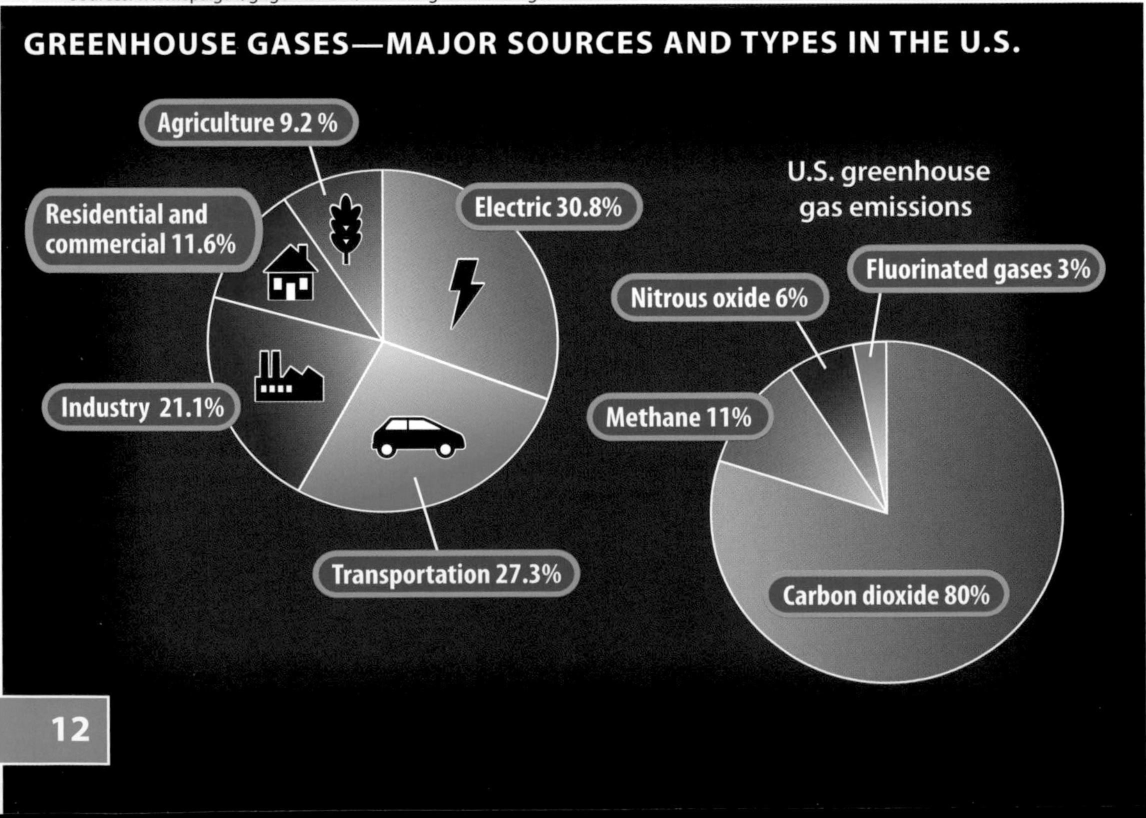

GREENHOUSE GASES—MAJOR SOURCES AND TYPES IN THE U.S.

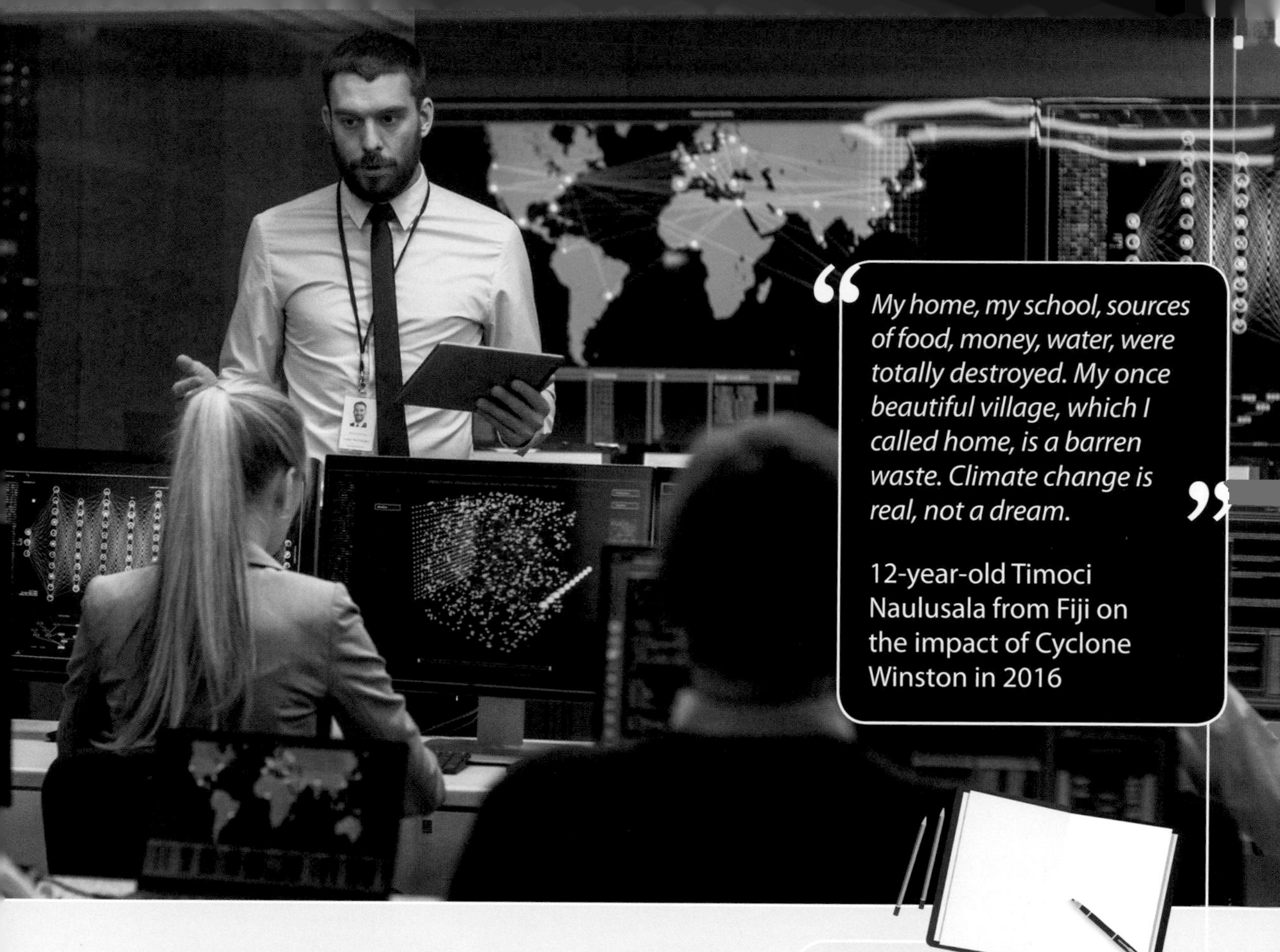

My home, my school, sources of food, money, water, were totally destroyed. My once beautiful village, which I called home, is a barren waste. Climate change is real, not a dream.

12-year-old Timoci Naulusala from Fiji on the impact of Cyclone Winston in 2016

Some people do not believe climate change is real or that taking action against it is a bad choice. During his 2016 election **campaign**, U.S. President Donald Trump claimed wind power was expensive and that many eagles die flying into wind turbines.

When researching climate change, use different **media**—websites, newspapers, TV, books—and look for up-to-date material from different perspectives, including people who deny it is happening or believe its impact is small.

MAKING SENSE OF STATISTICS

Graphs, pie charts, and diagrams are useful tools to present climate change facts and explain complex ideas. You need to learn how to interpret these visual forms of information. They can draw your attention to details, connections, and trends you may not otherwise notice.

ASK YOUR OWN QUESTIONS

To determine if a source is credible, consider:

- Does the creator have solid credentials and expertise in the topic?
- Does the headline match the story?
- Is the publisher known to be reliable?
- What sources did the creator use?
- Is the source relevant and up to date?
- Is the source meant to be a joke or **clickbait**?

3 THE BIG PICTURE

Scientists have been studying and writing reports about climate change for centuries. So why are people so much more worried about it today than they were in the past? To understand any issue, you need answers to the five Ws and an H—what, when, why, where, who, and how. Journalists, documentary makers, and other content creators use these questions to guide their work.

A component of Earth's atmosphere is the gas carbon dioxide (CO_2). A change in its levels in the atmosphere is the main cause of climate change. Earth's climate is always changing—it is a natural process that occurs over time. In fact, there have been times in the past when Earth's climate was much warmer—and also colder—than it is today. Sometimes, these changes in Earth's average climate last for thousands of years.

▼ At international climate change conventions, conferences, and summits around the world, members of the media deliver coverage of them to people globally.

NATURAL AND UNNATURAL CHANGE

Over the past 650,000 years, there have been several major global climate events such as ice ages. However, since the start of the **Industrial Revolution**, people have affected climate change in an unnatural way. Global warming refers to the gradual increase in temperature of Earth's air and oceans due largely to human activity, especially burning fossil fuels such as oil, gas, or coal.

Greenhouse gases are gases in the atmosphere that trap heat. They include carbon dioxide and water vapor. These are stored in Earth's rocks, oceans, and trees. Greenhouse gases help keep heat inside Earth's atmosphere so the planet is warm enough to support living things. This is known as the greenhouse effect, and it is a natural process that has happened since the start of time.

ASK YOUR OWN QUESTIONS

What—what is the issue?
When—when did it happen? Is it still taking place? Are there significant dates, times, and events?
Why—why is it happening and why does it matter?
Where —where is it taking place?
Who—who is involved? Who does it affect?
How—how does it affect life on the planet?

A NEW APPROACH

In the past, the media often used **doomsday** footage and reports of extreme climate conditions to shock viewers and readers. They focused on dramatic stories and talked about the uncertainty of climate change research.

In recent years, the media has started using a different approach to how they cover the issue. They now acknowledge the problem and express a need to take action to reduce **emissions** caused by human activities. They talk about technologies and ways to help reduce or eliminate global warming. They show the impact climate change has on people's daily lives, so everyone can see the benefit of making changes and taking action.

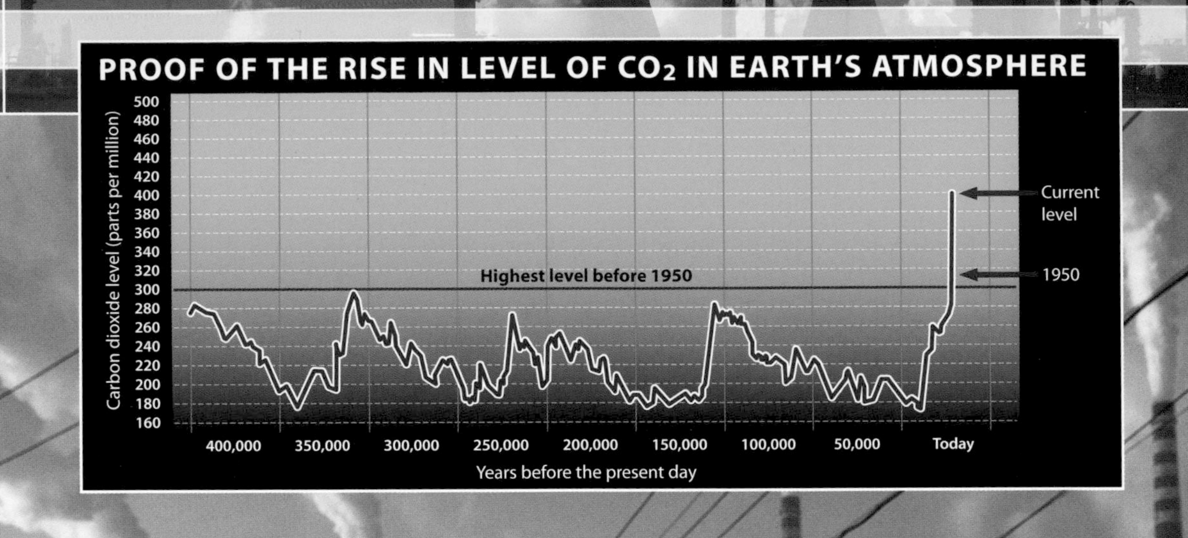

THE CENTRAL ISSUES

The rising average temperature of Earth's climate shows itself in different ways. In some places, it has a cooling effect while in other places it has a warming effect. Do you think this is why many scientists prefer the term "climate change" over "global warming"? Do you understand the difference between the two? Is there a danger of these terms being misused and why?

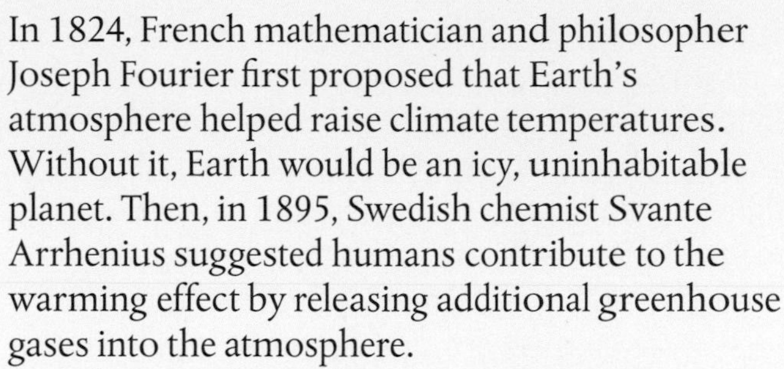

◄ Smoke billows from the chimneys of fossil fuel-powered factories in China. China is the world's major producer of greenhouse gases. Of these, there is 42 percent more carbon dioxide in the atmosphere today than there was before the start of the Industrial Revolution in the 1700s.

In 1824, French mathematician and philosopher Joseph Fourier first proposed that Earth's atmosphere helped raise climate temperatures. Without it, Earth would be an icy, uninhabitable planet. Then, in 1895, Swedish chemist Svante Arrhenius suggested humans contribute to the warming effect by releasing additional greenhouse gases into the atmosphere.

Volcanoes, bursts of energy from the Sun, and ocean currents all change the amounts of greenhouse gases in the atmosphere. But they do not typically have a lasting effect. We burn fossil fuels to heat and cool homes and buildings, drive vehicles and fly airplanes, and cut down forests. These and other human consumption habits change the level of carbon dioxide in the atmosphere at an unnatural rate. As a result, the atmosphere has become a massive heat-trapping blanket.

While the level of greenhouse gases in Earth's atmosphere has gone up and down over time, it was more or less stable for several thousand years. Recently, however, small yet significant changes have occurred. Earth's average temperature increased as much as 1.6 degrees Fahrenheit (0.9 degrees C) from 1906 to 2005.

SMALL CHANGE BUT GLOBAL IMPACT

Even the smallest changes in Earth's climate can have a severe impact. Ice sheets are melting in Greenland, the Arctic, and Antarctica; oceans are heating up; and sea levels are rising. Extreme weather events are affecting people on all continents. As oceans warm, there are less krill, and populations of birds and marine creatures that rely on them have declined. Walruses, seals, polar bears, and birds that live on sea ice are struggling to survive. Warmer weather leads to higher risk of forest fires and insect infestations.

Climate change has an **economic**, environmental, and social impact. Natural habitats are both changing in size and shifting position, causing some species of plants and animals to die off. Storms are causing flash floods in some locations. Many homes are destroyed and people are left with no place to live. Warmer climates are causing droughts in other places. There, people and crops cannot get enough water. Farmers are unable to grow enough food for local populations. **Malnutrition** and heat-related deaths are on the increase.

Climate patterns show Africa will be hardest hit by climate change. Much of the continent does not have the resources to cope with the impact. Scientists predict that between 75 and 250 million people in Africa will face a severe water shortage by 2020. Production of crops that rely on rain to grow will have decreased by as much as 50 percent by that same year.

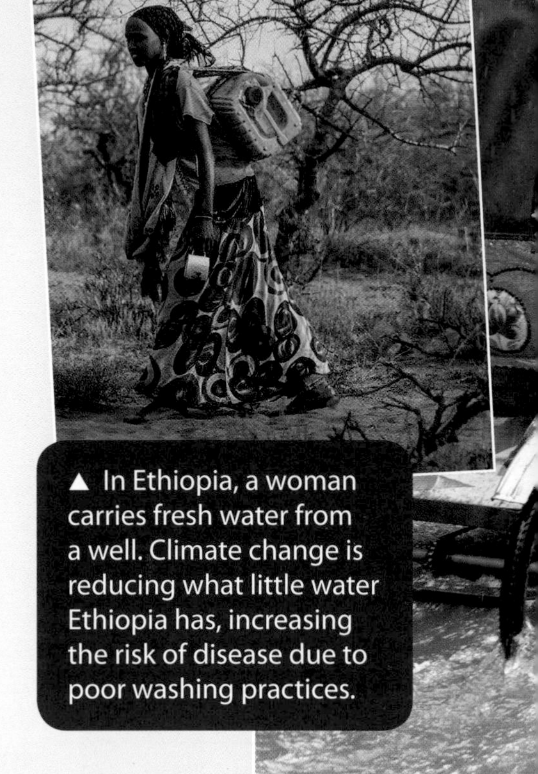

▲ In Ethiopia, a woman carries fresh water from a well. Climate change is reducing what little water Ethiopia has, increasing the risk of disease due to poor washing practices.

◀ Climate change is making wildfires more extreme by changing weather patterns and slowing the jet stream. The slowing means weather systems stay in the same place longer.

▲ Monsoon rain in Bangladesh. While the country is prone to natural disasters, such as floods, cyclones, and droughts, the frequency and severity of these events in recent years have become more intense due to climate change.

A MAJOR THAW

In northern regions, such as Canada's Northwest Territories, thawing **permafrost** is causing major damage to **infrastructure**. Buildings and roads built on what was a solid layer of frozen earth are now sinking into the soft ground. The damage tallies more than $50 million each year.

Scientists estimate approximately 20 percent of the permafrost will thaw by 2040. Plants and animals will need to adapt to the new conditions or migrate. A vast amount of fresh water will be unlocked. In addition, billions of tons of greenhouse gases stored inside the permafrost will be released into the environment, further increasing the impact of global warming.

LOW RISK
HIGH RISK

WHAT'S AT STAKE?

How do you think climate change will affect people and animals in North America? In what ways will its impact be similar in other continents?

If climate change is a natural process, why is it considered a problem and why should you get informed about it? What happened to shift our perspective on the topic? In the 1970s, scientists established that the **ozone layer** of Earth's atmosphere was getting thinner. The layer protects Earth from the harmful effects of the Sun's **ultraviolet** (**UV**) rays. It was revealed that human-made chemicals called chlorofluorocarbons (CFCs) used in spray cans and refrigerants, were making the ozone layer thinner and putting holes in it. Something had to be done to protect life on Earth.

Scientists presented the findings to politicians. It took until 1985 for countries all over the world to agree to cooperate on research. In 1987, they signed the Montreal Protocol on Substances that Deplete the Ozone Layer. The Montreal Protocol reduced 95 percent of CFCs and ozone depleting chemicals. By 2018, scientists could see that the ozone was beginning to repair itself.

HOT TOPIC

The Montreal Protocol proved that countries around the world could work together to improve Earth's environment. In 1988, the United Nations (UN) declared climate change, "A common concern for all mankind." By the 1990s, government agencies and environmental groups were doing research and developing **policies**. Despite overwhelming scientific agreement that global warming exists and it is being accelerated by human activity, there are naysayers who simply do not agree with the science. Others are **skeptical**: They are not convinced humans play a role in climate change.

KEY PLAYERS

António Manuel de Oliveira Guterres is a Portuguese politician and the Secretary-General of the United Nations. He is a staunch believer that the increased speed with which Earth's climate is changing is directly related to human activity. He has called upon world leaders to rise up against climate change and take action in their own countries.

▶ A panel on climate change meets in Paris in 2018. International cooperation has succeeded in reducing damage to the ozone layer from the use of chlorofluorcarbons (CFCs) released into the atmosphere. This reduction proves that taking action on climate change can work.

▶ The loss of sea ice due to climate change is a major threat to polar bears. The species could become extinct by 2100 if the ice continues to melt at the same rate as today.

4 INFORMATION LITERACY

Knowing when you need information, where to find it, how to evaluate if it is credible or not, and how to use it effectively are skills known as information literacy. Information comes from a variety of sources, including the media, friends, nonprofit groups, and scientists. In many cases, the information is unfiltered or unedited. How can you tell if the source of the information is reliable and accurate?

"It ain't what you don't know that gets you into trouble. It's what you know for sure that just ain't so."

U.S. Author Mark Twain

▶ According to the National Center for Science Education (NCSE), about 75 percent of middle and high school teachers provided information about climate change during the 2014 to 2015 school year. About 25 percent of them also gave students time to think about different perspectives that raise doubt about climate change.

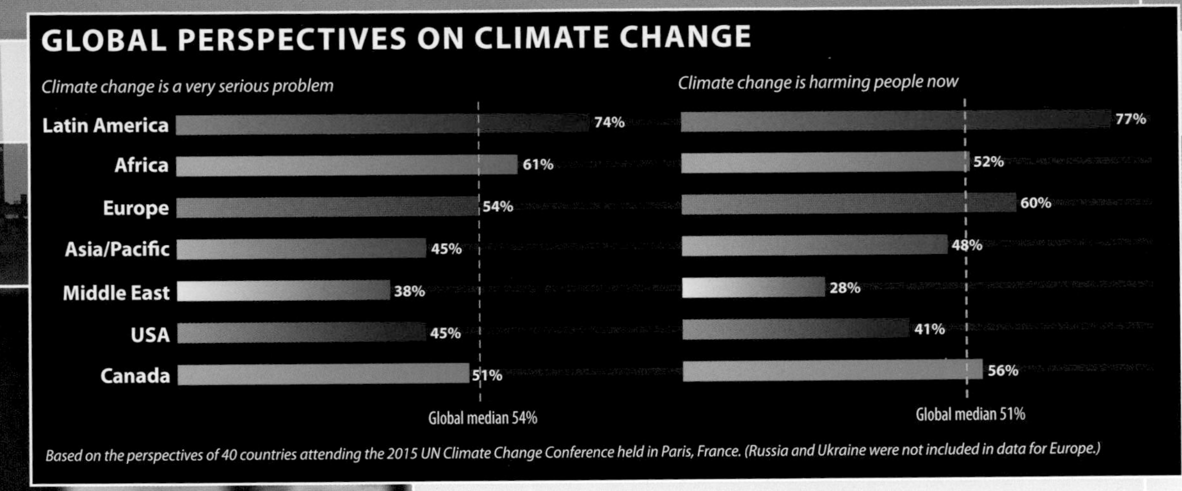

A STEP-BY-STEP PROCESS

A lot of what we see, read, or hear includes false information, leading us to form incorrect opinions and conclusions or become skeptical. Some information, such as statistics and diagrams, includes complex concepts and theories that are difficult to interpret. To be a lifelong learner, you need to develop information literacy skills so you can build awareness and draw reasonable conclusions based on facts and evidence.

To develop your information literacy skills regarding climate change, follow these steps:

- Figure out how much information you need. Ask yourself a question such as, "How can I tell if climate change is real?"
- Look for sources of information that can help answer this—government reports, podcasts, documentary films, science magazines, and science research databases are a few of the resources you can use.
- **Evaluate** each resource critically. Think about who made it: Did they talk about facts or include bias? Who was their main audience? Did they leave out any details?
- Put the information into your own words. Think about how you would express it if you were writing a blog post or giving a presentation.

Climate change can be viewed from many perspectives. For scientists, it is matter of physics and chemistry. Governments consider the economic and environmental aspects. Industry looks at it as business. Biologists look at its impact on living things.

Climate change deniers may ignore or oppose the science for several reasons. For example, many large companies depend on fossils fuels to fund or power their business. In addition, many western economies are often built on fossil fuel production and use. Their entire way of life is built on it. If they agree that human activity contributes to climate change, they would be expected to do something about it. That kind of widespread change puts their lifestyle at risk and could cost large amounts of money to implement. As a result, some try to **discredit,** devalue, or overlook scientific evidence of climate change.

CONFLICTING VIEWPOINTS

Some people are skeptics: They have experienced cold weather and think it means climate change has stopped. Some deniers think the people reporting the facts are part of a **conspiracy** to prevent them from living free.

To understand perspective, you need to imagine yourself in the same position as these people and consider how they would think, feel, or act to meet their objectives or expectations. It will open your mind to conflicting views.

SCIENTISTS SPEAK OUT

When we look at climate change from the scientific perspective, there is no denying the evidence. Several organizations have done studies of scientific research papers and reports published in a wide variety of technical journals. Their analysis shows 97 percent of scientists openly agree climate change is due—at least in part—to human activity. The remaining 3 percent of scientists simply did not state an opinion. Where some scientists do disagree is the impact and outcome of climate change.

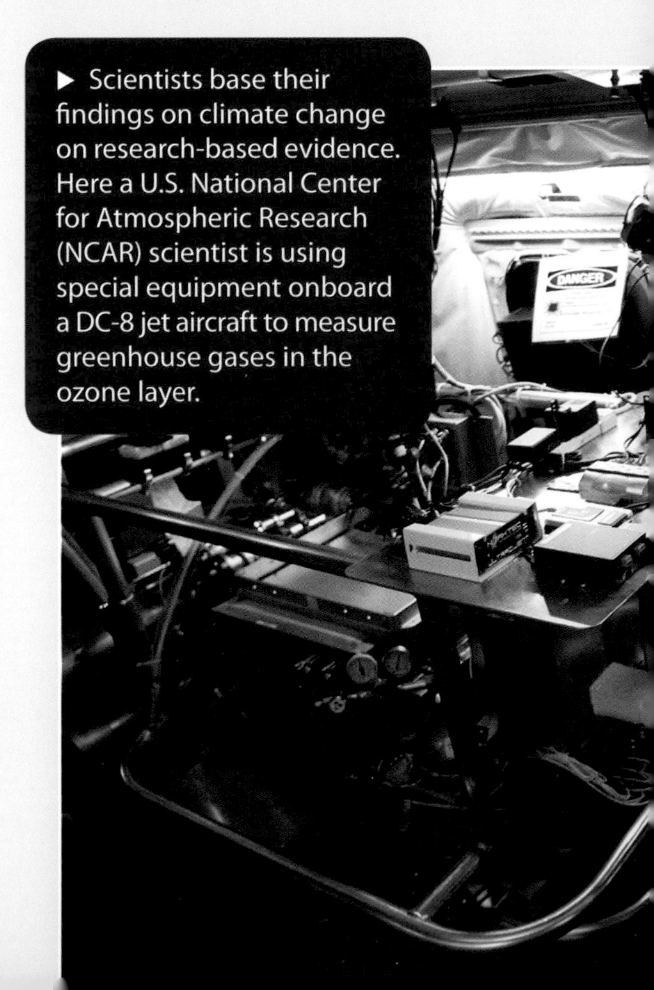

▶ Scientists base their findings on climate change on research-based evidence. Here a U.S. National Center for Atmospheric Research (NCAR) scientist is using special equipment onboard a DC-8 jet aircraft to measure greenhouse gases in the ozone layer.

SCIENTISTS’ VIEWS OF THE HUMAN ROLE IN GLOBAL WARMING

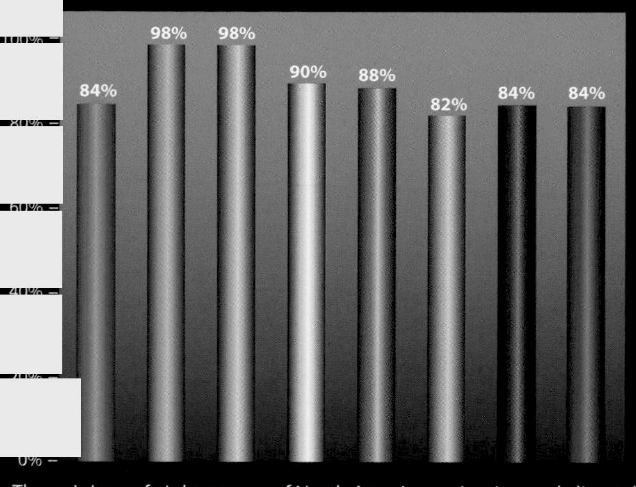

- Medical scientists
- 200 Most-published climate scientists
- Most frequently published climatologists
- Scientists publishing on climate change
- Climatologists
- Earth science faculty/researchers
- Climate scientists
- Geophysical scientists

The opinions of eight groups of North American scientists and climatologists—those supporting the theory.

KEY PLAYERS

Michael Bloomberg is a wealthy American businessman and politician. He served three terms as mayor of New York City. Bloomberg is also a well-known environmentalist. He has donated millions of dollars to climate change action programs run by environmental groups. Bloomberg was appointed by the United Nations twice as an envoy, or representative, for climate change. In 2017, he co-wrote a best-selling book called *Climate of Hope* on what can be done to stop climate change.

GLOBAL PERSPECTIVE

The Paris international climate agreement created in 2015 aims to minimize the global temperature rise to about 2.7 degrees Fahrenheit (1.5°C). This is because a 3.6 degrees Farhrenheit (2°C) difference would be globally catastrophic. To make this goal a reality, carbon emissions need to decline by 4 to 6 percent each year for many decades. Many nations need to make drastic changes to the way they do things, which could have severe economic and social impacts. Nearly every nation in the world is committed to working together under the agreement to combat climate change. The United States signed the agreement under President Barack Obama's leadership.

THE CENTRAL ISSUES

How may the U.S. economy change if the country has to dramatically reduce its use of fossil fuels? What other sources of energy could be used instead? Could these power factories and public transportation?

▶ A massive solar power plant in China, built to reduce the country's dependence on fossil fuels

> *NBC News just called it the great freeze—coldest weather in years. Is our country still spending money on the GLOBAL WARMING HOAX?*
>
> Donald Trump in a 2014 tweet

In 2017, President Trump said it was to his nation's benefit to withdraw from the agreement since the country relies so heavily on fossil fuels. The U.S. has now stated it will leave. President Trump has also said on numerous occasions that he is a climate change skeptic.

Countries including Denmark, China, France, India, and Sweden are investing heavily in combating climate change. Starting in 2008, Denmark began putting into place changes to reduce energy consumption and increase reliance on renewable energy sources. It is on target to eliminate fossil fuels use by 2050.

REACHING THE TARGET

China is the largest producer of carbon dioxide emissions and, until recently, was in denial about climate change. However, extreme weather conditions and high levels of smog caused the Chinese government to change its stance. In 2009, it announced plans to reduce its carbon emissions by as much as 45 percent by 2020. In 2017, China introduced an emissions trading scheme (ETS). The ETS includes putting a cap, or limit, on carbon emissions. It also allows industries to buy allowances that permit them to emit more carbon or sell their allowances to others when they emit less. This is called cap and trade. A cap and trade system was used to successfully cut **sulphur dioxide** emissions and curb **acid rain** in North America in the 1980s.

◄ Offshore wind turbines near Copenhagen, Denmark. Wind turbines currently supply 45 percent of Denmark's energy needs. That number is expected to increase to 60 percent in the next few years.

NONPROFIT ORGANIZATIONS' VIEWS

Many nonprofit organizations are formed to bring about change in government plans and actions and act as guardians of the planet. Regarding climate change, they may spend their time and money on efforts to slow or stop global warming. They fund projects and campaigns that promote climate change action in everyone's best interests. Nonprofit organizations include ConservAmerica, Canada's Environmental Defence, and Friends of the Earth.

▶ As part of a WWF campaign, papier-mâché models of pandas fill a pedestrian area of Bangkok, Thailand, to raise awareness of conservation of this endangered species. The forests in China that are home to pandas are being damaged or destroyed, threatening panda survival but also changing carbon dioxide levels in the atmosphere.

TAKING ACTION

International nonprofit climate change groups such as 350.org believe people are stronger when they collaborate. Through online campaigns and mass public demonstrations, 350.org works in 188 countries to discourage the funding of new fossil fuel projects and encourage companies to build 100-percent clean energy solutions. It also supports local communities that are struggling to cope with climate change problems.

Since it was established in 1892, the Sierra Club has become one of the largest environmental protection groups in the United States. Like 350.org, the group promotes moving away from using fossil fuels to power our world and looks for clean energy solutions instead.

Greenpeace and the World Wildlife Fund (WWF) draw awareness to the global impact of climate change. Their goal is to build a healthier future for ecosystems, and human populations.

Since nonprofit organizations are not driven by the need to make a money for profit, they can challenge myths and misconceptions about climate change. They can also question the accuracy of data that may be biased, and serve as an independent voice at global climate summits.

WHAT'S AT STAKE?

Nonprofit organizations, such as Greenpeace, often take direct action to bring about change. Some of their activists have been fined and imprisoned for the damage and disruption they have caused. Should the activists be doing this? How can people best put pressure on those held responsible for climate change?

▼ Greenpeace activists protest during a G20 meeting in Bonn, Germany. The regular meeting of 20 governments from around the world discusses global economy, including energy production and use.

BIG-INDUSTRY PERSPECTIVES

Many industries create carbon emissions and other pollutants as **byproducts** of their work. Mining companies, power stations, forestry organizations, car, train, and aircraft manufacturers, and many more stand to lose billions of dollars if they shut down operations or adopt climate-friendly practices. In the 1990s, oil and gas companies began spending millions of dollars funding campaigns that cast doubt on climate change. They formed **front groups** and **think tanks** that raised questions about scientific theories. They challenged scientists' data and government policies that threatened their findings and ways of working.

ASK YOUR OWN QUESTIONS

To pay for new environmentally friendly technologies and practices, energy costs will rise. Developing countries will need financial support from developed countries to put new systems in place. Would you as a taxpayer be willing to help pay for this?

NEW WAYS OF WORKING

Today, most major industries acknowledge a need to change their manufacturing processes and ways they do business to help prevent climate change. In many parts of the world, industries face enormous consequences, such as huge fines, for not meeting local climate policies.

These modifications and shifts in practices often cost industries a lot of money to develop new technologies and novel ways of doing things, such as **carbon capture and storage** and **sequestering**, which prevent carbon dioxide from being released back into the atmosphere. In addition, not only will the companies likely experience a great reduction in their profits, but also the economies of countries such as Canada, China, South Africa, and Brazil face harsh setbacks by loss of industry due to global climate change policies.

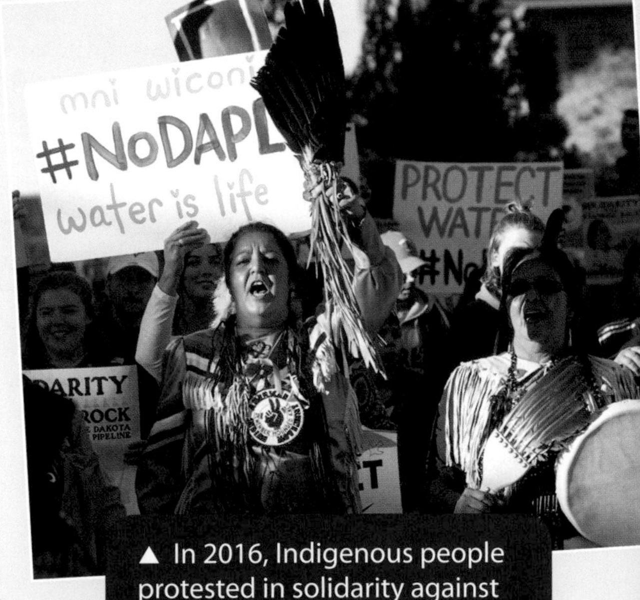

▲ In 2016, Indigenous people protested in solidarity against an oil pipeline running through Indigenous lands. The pipeline would make it easier and cheaper to supply oil refineries, but at a cost to the environment.

SHARED RESPONSIBILITY

Some energy companies, among them BP, Exxon, and Shell, have accepted the science and put action plans in place to reduce their carbon emissions. As respected industry leaders, they can no longer deny the facts. However, most have also pushed some of the responsibility back on society to help solve the problem. They have stated that a major cultural shift needs to occur to make any great progress. Consumers will need to curb their use of carbon-based products and governments will need to implement nationwide policies.

Environmentally friendly initiatives are now being used across the world. The transportation industry is moving toward the use of electric vehicles, and commuters are being encouraged to give up their cars and use trains, buses, bicycles, or even walk to work. Buildings are now constructed with better insulation and energy-saving devices. Digital technology is being used to run machinery and household appliances only when essential.

▲ Zero-carbon emissions technology is being used at Russia's Prirazlomnaya Arctic offshore oil rig to help prevent production and drilling waste from making its way into the sea and polluting it.

Though early industry initiatives to combat climate change seemed to be in the public interest, they sometimes tried to convince politicians and the media that global warming was not real. They said scientists did not understand climate change any better than the general public. This tactic worked for a long time, but as people have become more aware of the issue, they are raising questions of their own, forcing companies to rethink their strategy.

In recent years, public opinion has shifted away from disbelief and skepticism. In fact, 60 percent of American citizens believe climate change is already having an impact on our planet. Still, nearly half of all them do not think it will have a serious impact in their lifetime. About one-third of the population is not sure where they stand on the issue or do not spend much time thinking about it. Global public opinion on climate change varies greatly (see page 37).

POLITICAL DIVIDE

Nonbelievers, skeptics, and those who believe but do not care are often influenced by their leaders. They believe what their politicians are saying. In the United States, **Gallup polls** show 69 percent of **Republican** voters believe the seriousness of climate change is exaggerated or overstated compared to only 4 percent of **Democratic** voters. In Canada, the Green Party is far more committed to action against climate change than other parties in government.

To change public opinion, people need to see the impact climate change has on them personally. They need to see how health problems and air pollution are linked to climate change, and what they can do to help the issue.

▲ In 2006, the documentary *An Inconvenient Truth*, was made about the campaign of former U.S. Vice President Al Gore to highlight climate change to the general public. It was highly successful and is used in schools around the world.

> *"Whether you're a skeptic or a true believer in technology…we need a market in the transition to a low carbon future."*
>
> Mark Carney, Governor of the Bank of England, U.K., and Chair of the G20's Financial Stability Board

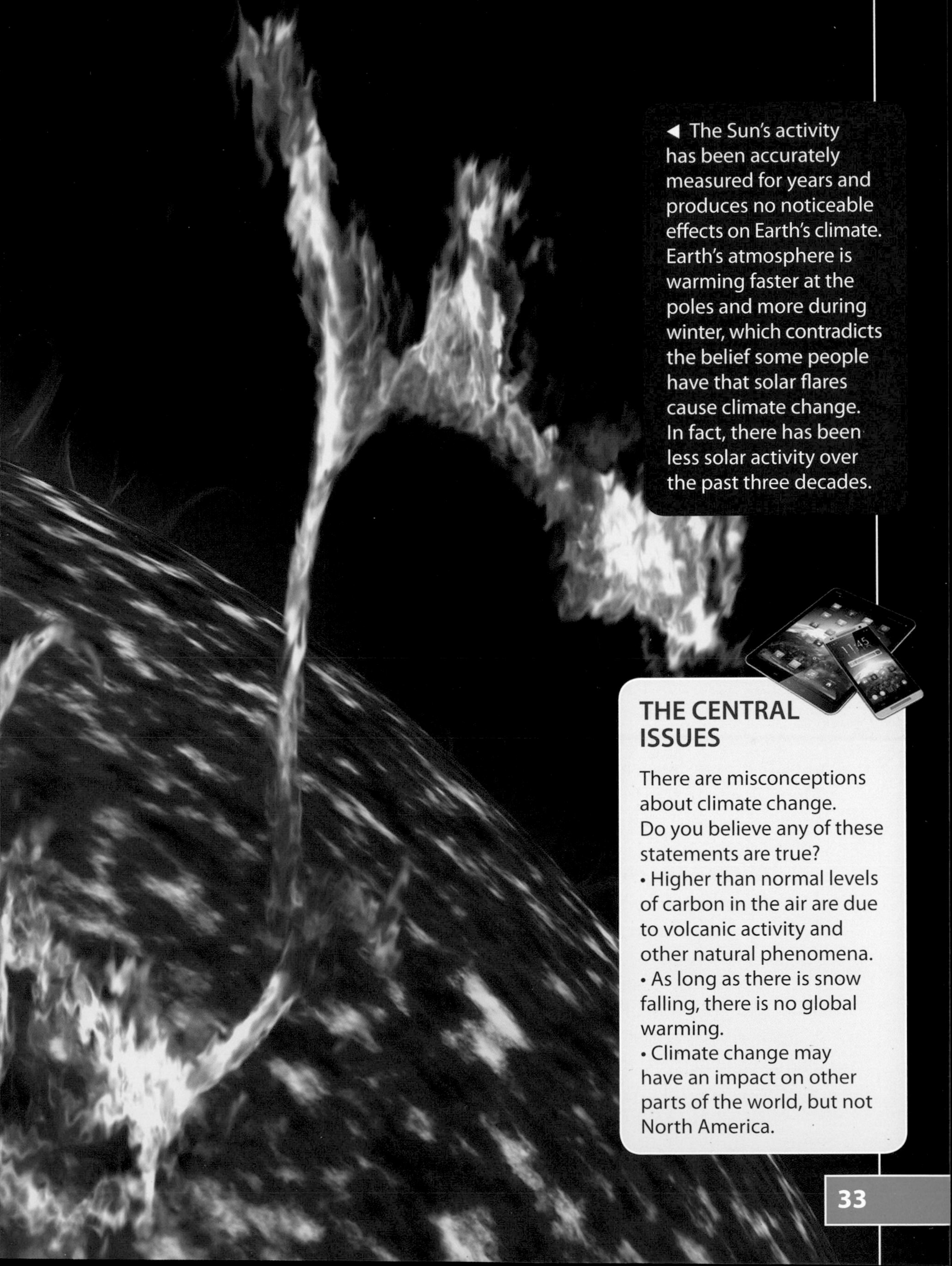

◀ The Sun's activity has been accurately measured for years and produces no noticeable effects on Earth's climate. Earth's atmosphere is warming faster at the poles and more during winter, which contradicts the belief some people have that solar flares cause climate change. In fact, there has been less solar activity over the past three decades.

THE CENTRAL ISSUES

There are misconceptions about climate change. Do you believe any of these statements are true?

- Higher than normal levels of carbon in the air are due to volcanic activity and other natural phenomena.
- As long as there is snow falling, there is no global warming.
- Climate change may have an impact on other parts of the world, but not North America.

5 STAYING INFORMED

You need to make careful choices when it comes to staying informed. From books, websites, and newspapers to podcasts, blogs, and science journals, there are thousands of source materials about climate change. Be sure to read and study a wide variety of materials from different sources, both historic and up-to-date. Over time, our understanding of a subject can change. People who once opposed the idea of climate change support the cause today and vice versa. As we learn more about a topic, and new events occur or scientific evidence is found, they can impact what we once thought to be true.

▲ Volcanic activity is known to spark climate change. Vast clouds of dust and gases are released into the atmosphere.

◀ Petrochemical plants use vast amounts of energy to convert natural resources into products widely used in industry. The global economy depends on them but they contribute to climate change. New technologies will, it is hoped, reduce their impact on the environment.

GOOD SOURCES OF INFORMATION

When researching a topic, be mindful of bias and misinformation. Thanks in part to the Internet and the power of social media, inaccurate details spread quickly. If a report appears extreme or does not make sense, compare it with other sources to determine if it is based on current, accurate facts. Check to see that the person who created the source is an authority on the issue, or uses statistics and facts to back up the information. Some good starter source materials for climate change will be found at:

- government environmental organizations such as the U.S. Environmental Protection Agency (EPA) and Environment Canada
- nonprofit groups such as the Center for Climate and Energy Solutions, Clean Foundation, Union of Concerned Scientists, and Idle No More
- respected environment, science, and climate experts, including Dr. David Suzuki, Dr. Syukuro Manabe, and Johan Rockström
- fact-based news media such as the British Broadcasting Corporation (BBC), National Public Radio (NPR), and C-SPAN
- documentaries such as *An Inconvenient Truth*
- grandparents and other senior members of the community who may have observed climate change over time
- podcasts such as *Science Vs* and *Yale Climate Connections*
- blog sites such as NASA's Earth Right Now.

Selected climate changes sources used in this book are listed on pages 46-47.

WHAT'S AT STAKE?

Have you noticed any effects of climate change—for example, more extreme weather conditions, and plants flowering and birds nesting earlier in the year? Imagine how these affect farming and wildlife populations on a local, national, and international scale.

Our understanding of the planet is always growing, as is our knowledge of how we are changing it. Most of the global warming caused by humans has happened over the past 30 to 40 years. Since 2001, we have seen the warmest climate temperatures on record for 16 out of 17 years. Oceans have absorbed most of the heat, and, in parts of the world, glaciers are retreating.

In 2017, scientists discovered Earth's polar ice regions are melting twice as fast as they previously thought. Arctic ice is melting at its fastest rate in the past 1,500 years or more. For several years in a row, the North Pole has had a heat wave in the middle of winter, leading to much lower levels of sea ice than normal.

Over the past few years, we have seen extreme weather conditions around the world. Australia and Argentina have experienced intense heat waves. Kenya and Somalia have faced severe droughts. Sri Lanka has been hit hard by landslides and flooding due to heavy rains. Massive hurricanes, such as Harvey and Maria, pummeled the North American Atlantic Coast and Caribbean in autumn 2017. Scientists say this is just a glimpse of what the future will hold as global warming becomes worse over time.

INTO THE FUTURE

At the 2018 World Economic Forum (WEF), the lack of climate change action was identified as one of the major risks to global **prosperity**. Similarly, the WEF's *The Global Risk Report 2018* lists the environment as the world's greatest concern today. WEF experts agree the world is at risk of extreme weather events and major natural disasters. There is also the risk of **biodiversity** loss and ecosystems being destroyed.

KEY PLAYERS

The World Economic Forum has been working to improve the world since 1971. Located in Geneva, Switzerland, WEF is an **impartial** organization with no political ties or special interests. It works with global leaders and experts in the areas of business, politics, and industry for the greater good of the public at large.

> *Climate change is intrinsically linked to public health, food and water security, migration, peace, and security. It is a moral issue. It is an issue of social justice, human rights and fundamental ethics. We have a profound responsibility to the fragile web of life on this Earth, and to this generation and those that will follow.*
>
> Former United Nations Secretary-General Ban Ki-moon

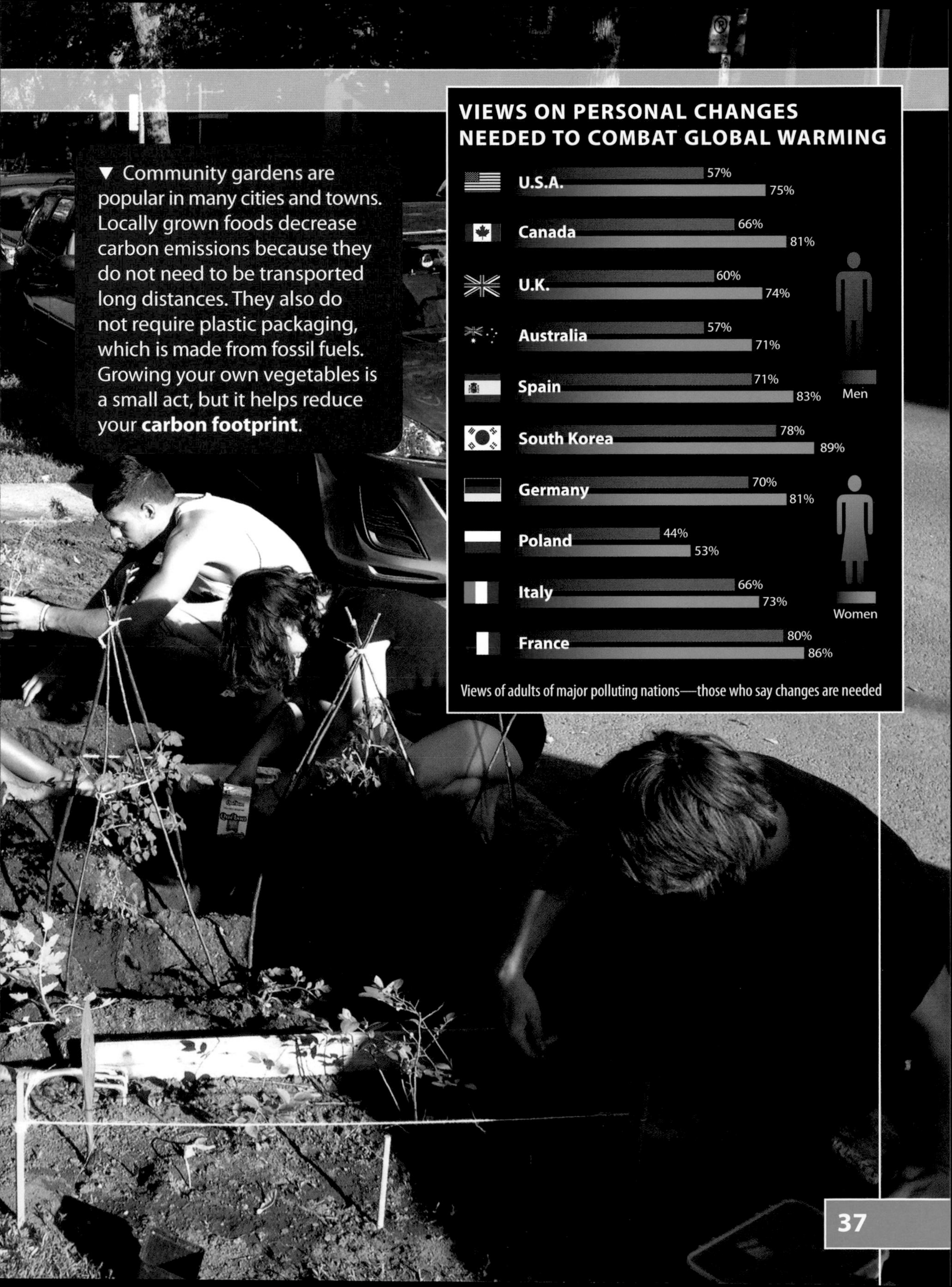

▼ Community gardens are popular in many cities and towns. Locally grown foods decrease carbon emissions because they do not need to be transported long distances. They also do not require plastic packaging, which is made from fossil fuels. Growing your own vegetables is a small act, but it helps reduce your **carbon footprint**.

FOLLOWING GLOBAL INITIATIVES

Most current news on climate change is about initiatives to reduce the human output of carbon dioxide from industry. Carbon dioxide emissions are at their highest levels in 800,000 years. The emissions we make today will remain in the atmosphere for thousands of years to come.

Fossil fuels still account for the majority of energy consumption around the world and will until at least 2040. To make the shift to **green energy** much easier, renewable energy costs have been greatly reduced in recent years.

FOLLOW THE MONEY

In India, pollution levels from vehicles and buildings are staggering. Millions of people die each year due to air quality issues. The air in the nation's capital, New Delhi, is so bad that breathing it in is equal to smoking 10 cigarettes a day. To help solve the issue, the government has vowed to sell only electric vehicles by 2030. China, home to the world's largest auto market, has plans to put five million electric cars on the road by 2020. In Europe, the United Kingdom, France, Norway, and at least eight other countries have set targets for the number of electric cars they want on the road by a given year.

The World Bank, an international financial institution that provides money to countries for large projects, is also jumping onboard to help reduce the growing threat caused by climate change. The bank announced it will no longer provide money for oil-and-gas exploration activities after 2019, except for extreme cases in the poorest developing countries where energy is in short supply. However, the projects must not conflict with climate change targets established as part of the Paris Climate Agreement.

WHAT'S AT STAKE?

In the United States, the frost-free growing season is already longer than it was in the 1980s. Since the 1900s, the average annual precipitation has increased. Heat waves and hurricanes are expected to become more intense, and you will begin to see less intense cool weather conditions. How do you think these changes will affect your life?

KEY PLAYERS

Angela Merkel became the first female chancellor of Germany in 2005 and is considered one of the most powerful women in the world. She is known as the Climate Chancellor for her persistent views on emissions cuts. Merkel took a lead role in creating the Paris Climate Agreement. Germany set an ambitious goal of reducing carbon emissions to below 40 percent of its 1990 levels by 2020. Germany will not likely meet this target, which could have a damaging effect on the nation's reputation as a climate leader.

◄ New York City is aiming to reduce emissions by as much as 80 percent by 2050.

◄ Former U.S. Vice President Al Gore spoke about the documentary *An Inconvenient Sequel: Truth to Power,* during a question-and-answer session in London, England. The film follows Gore's efforts to persuade governments to invest in renewable energy sources.

6 PLAN OF ACTION

Information is like food. You should eat a variety of meals with nutritious fruits and vegetables to keep your body healthy. Fast foods are quick and easy, but they can have a negative impact on your health. Similarly, a diet of information from reputable organizations can help you build a healthy perspective of world issues. Blogs and social media sites, such as Facebook and Twitter, feed you with a constant stream of news. The news is fast and easy to access, but it may include biased or false information that can lead you to make poor decisions. So be selective about the information you consume.

▶ Television news stations around the world, such as N24 in Germany, share the local perspective on global issues.

INTERNET SEARCHES

When looking at websites, address extensions can help identify the sources of the information.

.gov (government)—official government organizations or departments. You may not be able to access all areas of these websites.

.org usually non-profit organizations and charities. You may have to register to use these.

.com (commercial)—mostly businesses. It is the most widely used web address extension.

Country extensions:
.ca Canada
.us United States
.au Australia
.uk United Kingdom
.ru Russia
.de Germany

WHERE TO LOOK NOW

The status of the debate about climate change is likely to be very different tomorrow and in the future than it is today. To stay informed you must follow the work of scientists as they perform new experiments and make new discoveries.

On page 35 are listed sources of information you can use to *get* informed. Here are some sources and guidelines to help you *stay* informed.

- Read major newspapers and magazines from around the world, such as *The New York Times, The Washington Post, The Wall Street Journal,* and *Time,* in the United States, *The National Post, The Globe and Mail,* and *Maclean's* from Canada, and *New Scientist* and *The Economist* from the U.K.
- Watch streaming news programs on the Internet, such as *CNN News Student* and *Reuters,* and evening news programs on television. Be sure to include global programs, such as *BBC* in the U.K. and *W5* or *The Fifth Estate* in Canada.
- Have conversations with friends and family about current affairs.
- Listen to podcasts and radio shows, including programs that do not share your own point of view on the topic.
- Set up a Google alert for news stories about climate change so you never miss out on seeing the latest information.
- Follow scientists, world leaders, politicians, nonprofit organizations, and others on social media, such as Facebook and Twitter—being mindful to avoid clickbait.

With any topic you are researching, if a story sounds unrealistic or you are unsure about the source, be sure to fact check the details. Internet websites such as *FactCheck.org*'s SciCheck shine a spotlight on false information. The site reports on misleading stories people and organizations create to get your support. *Snopes.com* alerts you to misinformation, myths, and urban legends.

If the Internet is your main source of information, make sure the sites you visit are real. Lots of advertising or poor grammar may be a sign that the website is not a good source of information. There are other ways to tell, too. Many fake sites use a name similar to a brand name. Type the site into the Google search bar. If it is a real site, there should be links to it from other websites. You can also look to see if the site provides contact information. If there is only a form to fill out, it could be a sign the site is not real or is not regularly monitored and updated.

MAKE A CHANGE

Many people believe there is nothing ordinary citizens can do about climate change. In fact, there are lots of steps people can take to help reverse or limit the impact of climate change. Reducing waste by reusing or recycling goods is a great place to start. You can reduce emissions by walking or biking instead of taking a motorized vehicle. Turning off the lights when you leave a room, and purchasing energy-efficient appliances and vehicles, are other ways to reduce your family's carbon footprint. Encourage other people to do the same. While these acts may seem small, they can make a big difference over time. It may not be possible to reverse human impact on climate, but it can be better controlled.

▼ Getting informed and staying informed is vital when it comes to issues such as climate change. The time to act is now. The longer people wait to take action on climate change, the worse it will get and the harder it will be to reduce the impact.

ASK YOUR OWN QUESTIONS

Consider your climate change news diet:

- What news sources do you use daily?
- How long do you spend using each source?
- What did you learn?
- What trends did you see?

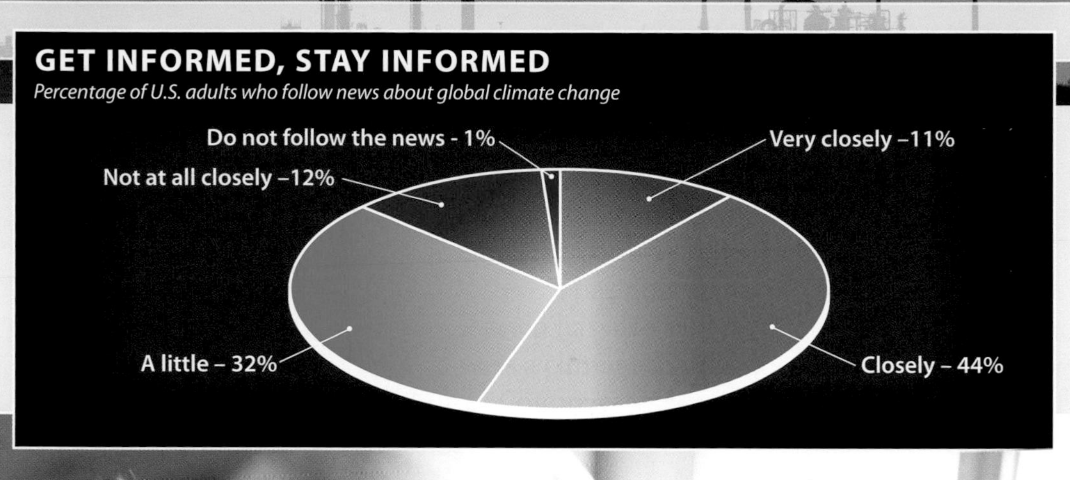

TAKE ACTION

Try these ideas to help you, your family, and your friends get informed and stay informed about climate change.

- Attend and participate in community meetings about what people can do and are doing to cut down their use of fossil fuels.
- Sign petitions supporting environmental projects in your community.
- Use social media to share facts and information about climate change's local, national, and international impacts.

GLOSSARY

acid rain Rain that has been made acidic from chemical pollution in the air. It is harmful to the environment.

analyzing Studying something carefully

atmosphere The layer of gases around Earth and other planets

biodiversity The variety of life

byproducts Unwanted items in a manufacturing process

campaign A plan with a goal or clear aim

carbon capture and storage The process of capturing carbon dioxide and storing it in a way so that it does not enter the atmosphere

carbon footprint The amount of carbon dioxide emitted by one's use of fossil fuels

clickbait Content that entices a person to click on a certain website or weblink

climate Long-term weather conditions on a large scale

conspiracy A theory that something occurred as a result of a secret plot

context Circumstances, background, or setting for an event or idea

controversy Disagreement over a certain matter

credible Able to be trusted or believed

current affairs Events happening now

debated Argued in a formal way

Democratic (people) People who support the U.S. Democratic political party

discredit To harm the reputation of someone or something

doomsday The last day on Earth; the end of the world

droughts Long-lasting periods of little rainfall, resulting in water shortages

economic Relating to the wealth and resources of a country

ecosystems Communities of living things in a specific environment

emissions Pollutants discharged into the atmosphere

evaluate Judge or determine the value of something

evidence Information or facts that prove if something is true or real

fossil fuels Natural fuels such as oil, gas, and coal, formed millions of years ago from the remains of dead animals

front groups Organizations that say they believe one thing but support something else

fundamentals Basics or component parts

Gallup polls Questions asked of people to find out their opinion

global warming Rise in temperature of Earth's atmosphere and oceans

green energy Energy that does little or no harm to the environrment

greenhouse effect Trapping heat in the atmosphere

hype Use of publicity and advertising to make people believe a certain thing

impartial Treating everyone equally

Industrial Revolution The rise of industry from the late 1700s to early 1800s

infrastructure Constructed systems such as road and rail networks

interpretations Explanations of the meanings of something

malnutrition Extremely poor nutrition due to the lack of a balanced diet

media Methods of mass communication such as television and radio

migration The act of moving from one place to another

myths Ideas that people believe, even if they are not true

observations Notes and recordings of things one has seen

ozone layer A layer in Earth's upper atmosphere that blocks many of the Sun's harmful rays

permafrost A permanently frozen layer of rock and soil

perspectives Viewpoints

policies Plans of action adopted by governments and organizations

prosperity Thriving or having a lot

renewable energy Energy that comes from sources that are naturally replaced

Republican (people) People who support the Republican Party

sequestering Setting apart or hiding away

skeptical Having doubts or not being easily convinced

statistics Math dealing with the collection, analysis, and presentation of numerical data

sulphur dioxide A gas produced when burning fossil fuels to produce energy. It creates acid rain.

summarizing Stating the main points briefly

think tanks Groups of experts who share ideas on an issue

ultraviolet (UV) Rays of energy from the Sun that are not visible to the human eye but that can cause damage to the skin

SOURCE NOTES

QUOTATIONS

p. 4 http://unfoundationblog.org/7-quotes-on-climate-change-and-health
p. 7 www.huffingtonpost.ca/entry/2016-republicans-climate-change_us_5654fd44e4b072e9d1c11291
p. 10 www.theguardian.com/environment/2017/nov/15/climate-change-will-determine-humanitys-destiny-says-angela-merkel
p. 13 https://cop23.com.fj/timoci-and-shalvi-fijis-youngest-climate-stars
p. 22 www.searchquotes.com/search/mark+twain
p. 32 www.climatechangenews.com/2018/01/23/davos-2018-climate-change-rhetoric-reality
p. 36 http://unfoundationblog.org/7-quotes-on-climate-change-and-health
p. 39 www.newsweek.comwhat-has-trump-said-about-global-warming-quotes-climate-change-paris-agreement-618898

REFERENCES USED FOR THIS BOOK

Chapter 1: Global Impact pp. 4-7
https://climate.nasa.gov/evidence
www.climaterealityproject.org/climate-101
www.skillsyouneed.com/learn/lifelong-learning.html
www.kidsdiscover.com/parentresources/9-tips-for-raising-lifelong-learners

Chapter 2: Approaching an Issue pp. 8-13
https://library.buffalo.edu/help/research-tips/background
http://researchguides.ben.edu/topics?p=2427767
www.bbc.com/news/science-environment-15874560
www.nottingham.ac.uk/studyingeffectively/reading/infotypes.aspx
https://fair.org/take-action-now/media-activism-kit/how-to-detect-bias-in-news-media
www.readingrockets.org/article/diagrams-timelines-and-tables

Chapter 3: The Big Picture pp. 14-21
https://its.unl.edu/bestpractices/remember-5-ws
https://climate.nasa.gov/evidence
www.climaterealityproject.org/climate-101
www.theozonehole.com
http://mpe.dimacs.rutgers.edu
www.cbc.ca/news/canada
www.unenvironment.org
www.canadiangeographic.ca
https://climateactionnetwork.ca
www.ipcc.ch
www.theozonehole.com
www.aljazeera.com

Chapter 4: Information Literacy pp. 22-33
www.cct.umb.edu/susjudgement.html
www.readingrockets.org/article/teaching-information-literacy-skills
http://climatecommunication.yale.edu
www.theccc.org.uk
www.ucsusa.org/global-warming
https://abcnews.go.com
www.skepticalscience.com
https://insideclimatenews.org/news
https://climateactiontracker.org
www.worldwildlife.org/initiatives/climate
www.sierraclub.org/about
https://350.org/about

Chapter 5: Staying Informed pp. 34-39
www.theguardian.com/environment
www.weforum.org
www.climaterealityproject.org/climate-101
www.usatoday.com
http://indianexpress.com
www.huffingtonpost.ca

Chapter 6: Plan of Action pp. 40-43
https://learning.blogs.nytimes.com
www.factcheck.org/scicheck
http://superheroyou.com/12-steps-to-becoming-well-informed
http://informationdiet.com
https://healthydemocracy.org
www.wikihow.com/Find-if-a-Website-Is-Legitimate
www.themuse.com/advice/staying-current-get-global-news-the-right-way

FIND OUT MORE

Finding good source material on the Internet can sometimes be a challenge. When analyzing how reliable the information is, consider these points:

- Who is the author of the page? Is it an expert in the field or a person who experienced the event?
- Is the site well known and up to date? A page that has not been updated for several years probably has out-of-date information.
- Can you verify the facts with another site? Always double-check information.
- Have you checked all possible sites? Don't just look on the first page a search engine provides.
- Remember to try government sites and research papers.
- Have you recorded website addresses and names? Keep this data so you can backtrack later and verify the information you want to use.

WEBSITES

Get the latest facts about climate change and how you can take action to help stop it.
https://climatekids.ca

Learn the science behind climate change and the greenhouse effect.
www.c2es.org/content/climate-basics-for-kids

Find out more about the impact of climate change and how to calculate your own emissions.
www3.epa.gov/climatechange//kids/index.html

BOOKS

DK Publishing. *Climate Change.* DK Eyewitness Books, 2008.

Heos, Bridget. *It's Getting Hot in Here: The Past, Present, and Future of Climate Change.* HMH Books for Young Readers, 2016.

Herman, Gail and Who HQ. *What Is Climate Change?* Penguin Workshop, 2018.

DOCUMENTARY FILMS

An Inconvenient Truth and *An Inconvenient Sequel: Truth to Power*

ABOUT THE AUTHOR

Heather C. Hudak has written hundreds of books for children. When she's not writing, Heather loves traveling and has been to more than 50 countries.

INDEX